OFFICIAL SQA PAST PAPERS WITH ANSWERS

STANDARD GRADE | GENERAL | CREDIT

COMPUTING STUDIES
2006-2010

© Scottish Qualifications Authority

First exam published in 2006.
Published by Bright Red Publishing Ltd, 6 Stafford Street, Edinburgh EH3 7AU
tel: 0131 220 5804 fax: 0131 220 6710 info@brightredpublishing.co.uk www.brightredpublishing.co.uk

ISBN 978-1-84948-084-0

A CIP Catalogue record for this book is available from the British Library.

Bright Red Publishing is grateful to the copyright holders, as credited on the final page of the book, for permission to use their material.
Every effort has been made to trace the copyright holders and to obtain their permission for the use of copyright material.
Bright Red Publishing will be happy to receive information allowing us to rectify any error or omission in future editions.

[BLANK PAGE]

FOR OFFICIAL USE

KU   PS

Total Marks

G

0560/402

NATIONAL QUALIFICATIONS 2006

THURSDAY, 11 MAY
G/C 9.00 AM – 10.15 AM
F/G 10.20 AM – 11.35 AM

COMPUTING STUDIES
STANDARD GRADE
General Level

Fill in these boxes and read what is printed below.

Full name of centre

Town

Forename(s)

Surname

Date of birth

Day Month Year   Scottish candidate number   Number of seat

Read each question carefully.

Attempt **all** questions.

Write your answers in the space provided on the question paper.

Write as neatly as possible.

Answer in sentences wherever possible.

Before leaving the examination room you must give this book to the invigilator. If you do not, you may lose all the marks for this paper.

SCOTTISH
QUALIFICATIONS
AUTHORITY

©

1. A new community centre is soon to open in the town of Bishophill. The manager is creating a web page to advertise the centre.

(a) Apart from text, name **two** other *types of data* which could be included in the web page.

_____

_____

(b) State **one** method which can be used to prepare web pages.

_____

_____

(c) The manager wants readers of the web page to be able to go directly to a page, which already exists, on the history of the town.

Describe **one** way in which this could be done.

_____

_____

(d) A group of school children are designing a logo for the community centre, using a drawing package. A line in the logo looked like this.

It has been changed to look like the one below.

What has happened to make this change?

_____

_____

KU | PS

1. (continued)

(*e*)   The community centre intends holding music evening classes.

Using the Internet, the manager wants to find out what other music evening classes are available in the town of Bishophill.

Tick (✓) the **one** option which would let him find this out most efficiently.

Use a search engine and search for evening classes.   ☐

Type in the individual address of each known evening class provider.   ☐

Use a search engine and search for music evening classes and Bishophill.   ☐

1
0

[Turn over

KU | PS

KU	PS

2. A letter is being sent out to everyone who has registered an interest in the community centre. The letter contains a *standard paragraph*.

(*a*) (i) What is a standard paragraph?

_____

_____

(ii) State **one** advantage of a standard paragraph.

_____

_____

(*b*) What feature of the word processing software would pick up the following underlined mistake?

The centre <u>are</u> having an opening ceremony on 27 September 2006.

_____

(*c*) The letter is to include a timetable of the various activities taking place in the community centre.

Describe **two** reasons why the *table* facility would prove useful in this situation.

1 _____

_____

2 _____

_____

(*d*) Page two of the letter starts in the middle of a paragraph.

What facility within a word processing package can be used to force the whole paragraph to move onto page two?

_____

_____

Margin marks: 2 1 0 (KU); 1 0 (KU); 1 0 (PS); 2 1 0 (PS); 1 0 (PS)

KU	PS

KU	PS

3. Below is a record from the database which holds details of people who have registered an interest in the community centre.

Registration Number	156
Name	Cameron Murray
Date of Birth	04/03/86
Sex	Male
Address line 1	13 Fauld Street
Address line 2	Bishophill
Postcode	BH3 82Y
Main Interest	Music

(a) Look at the above record and write down **two** *field types* that could be used in this database.

1 _____

2 _____

2
1
0

(b) What type of check could be done on the Date of Birth field to ensure that it falls within the years 1905 to 2006?

_____

1
0

(c) How could the database be used to identify the youngest person who has registered an interest in the community centre?

_____

_____

2
1
0

(d) Complete the following paragraph which describes how you would obtain a paper copy of people born after 01/07/85 and who are interested in music.

Perform a complex _____ on the "Date of Birth" field for a

date _____ 01/07/85 AND the _____ field

for "Music". Produce a paper copy using a _____ .

4
3
2
1
0

[Turn over

4. The manager of the community centre has made a spreadsheet of the various activities that are planned.

	A	B	C	D	E	F	G
1	Activity	Number of Participants	Cost per Participant	Total from Participants	Tutor Fee	Cost of Room	Profit
2	Beginners French	12	£55.55	£666.60	£200.00	£60.50	£406.10
3	5-a-side football	10	£20.00	£200.00	£50.00	£100.00	£50.00
4	Learn to play Guitar	6	£75.00	£450.00	£70.00	£60.50	£319.50
5	Painting	20	£35.00	£700.00	£200.00	£80.00	£420.00
6							
7							
8							
9	Maximum attending a class	20					
10	Average Tutor fee	£130.00					
11							

(*a*) What can be done to prevent the Tutor Fee from being changed accidentally?

_____

(*b*) Tick (✓) **one** box which gives the formula which is in G2.

= B2*C2   ☐

= D2−E2+F2   ☐

= D2+E2   ☐

= D2−E2−F2   ☐

(*c*) In cells B9 and B10 functions have been used. Fill in the spaces below with the functions and cell references in the appropriate places.

(i) B9   = _____ (_____ : _____)

(ii) B10 = _____ (_____ : _____)

(*d*) The manager wants a printout for the notice board of the number of people taking part in each activity.

State **one** reason why he might present the figures as a *chart* for this printout.

_____

_____

DO NOT
WRITE IN
THIS MARGIN

KU | PS

5. The manager of the community centre is working out a budget for the running of the office.

(a) Describe **two** *running costs* of computers.

1 _____

2 _____

2
1
0

(b) The manager also has to consider *security* with regard to the use of computers.
Suggest **two** methods which could be used to *control access* to the data held on computers.

1 _____

_____

2 _____

_____

2
1
0

(c) It can be argued that computers are expensive to buy. State **one** other disadvantage of introducing computers to an office.

_____

_____

1
0

[Turn over

6. Within the reception area of the community centre there is going to be a computer which runs an *expert system*. This expert system is to give advice as to which activities people may be interested in.

   (*a*)   (i) Where else might an expert system be used?

           _____

           _____

      (ii) What would it be used for in this situation?

           _____

           _____

   (*b*) People may wish to take a printout of the results from the expert system. The manager must purchase a new printer for this.

      Suggest **one** reason why he might choose to buy **each** of the following printers.

      Laser _____

      _____

      Inkjet _____

      _____

   (*c*) Expert systems are written in *high level languages*. Why is it necessary for high level languages to be *translated*?

      _____

      _____

   (*d*) Apart from translation, state **two** *common features* of high level languages.

      _____

      _____

      _____

      _____

Margin marks: (a)(i) 1 0 ; (a)(ii) 1 0 ; (b) 2 1 0 ; (c) 1 0 ; (d) 2 1 0

KU | PS

6.   (continued)

(e)   Live images of what is happening in reception are to be displayed on the community centre's web page.

Suggest an input device which could be used to capture these images.

_____

1
0

(f)   The computers in the community centre have *LCDs* which use *TFT* technology.

(i)   What do the initials LCD stand for?

L _____ C _____ D_____

1
0

(ii)   What do the initials TFT stand for?

T _____ F _____ T_____

1
0

[Turn over

7. When a person calls to book a place for an evening class, the receptionist checks the computer for availability and can respond by making the booking.

(a) What type of processing is this?

_____

(b) The centre creates a membership code for each member. Below is an example of a membership code and how it is created.

Write beside each one whether it is *data* or *information*.

(i) Code: CM1986M   _____

(ii) How it is created:

CM	1986	M
Initials	DOB	Sex

_____

(c) The membership code, shown above, is held in the community centre's computer.

Tick (✓) **one** box which describes how the membership code will be represented within the computer's memory.

Bitmap   ☐

ASCII   ☐

Graphics   ☐

(d) The person then sends in a cheque to pay for their evening class. The cheque contains *Magnetic Ink Character Recognition (MICR)* characters.

Describe **two** advantages of MICR.

1 _____

_____

2 _____

_____

7. **(continued)**

(e) Later that week the person goes on to their *on-line banking* to see whether the cheque has been taken off their bank balance. To access on-line banking a *password* must be used.

(i) Tick (✓) **one** box which best describes a safe and suitable password.

Your name ☐

Your date of birth ☐

A combination of letters and numbers ☐

Two letters of the alphabet ☐

(ii) State **one** reason why people using on-line banking should be glad of the Computer Misuse Act.

_____

_____

_____

(f) In years to come the community centre may expand greatly and require the services of a *Network Manager*.

Tick (✓) **one** box to indicate a specific duty of a Network Manager.

Deciding each user's level of access ☐

Writing a program ☐

Repairing a computer ☐

(g) The centre manager is worried about information stored in a database being lost or damaged.

What would you suggest he does?

_____

_____

[**Turn over**

KU	PS

7. (continued)

(*h*)   The manager uses both *data files* and *program files*. The membership file is a data file.

Tick (✓) the most appropriate definition for each.

(i)   **Program file**   A set of instructions   ☐

A file created by or used within a program   ☐

1
0

(ii)   **Data file**   A set of instructions   ☐

A file created or used within a program   ☐

1
0

KU	PS

KU	PS

8. When e-mailing tutors who are going to take classes at the community centre the manager must be aware of *netiquette*.

(*a*)   (i)   What is meant by the term *netiquette*?

_____

_____

1
0

(ii)   Give **two** examples of rules used in *netiquette*.

1 _____

_____

2 _____

_____

2
1
0

(*b*)   The manager currently uses a *dial-up connection* and wants to move to a *broadband connection*.

Give **two** advantages of using broadband.

1 _____

_____

2 _____

_____

2
1
0

[Turn over

KU	PS

9. The community centre will be holding a trip to a theme park. One of the rides involves passengers travelling back in time in a car (an automated vehicle) through Dinosaurland.

(a) One dinosaur breathes fire as it detects cars going past. Suggest a suitable device which could be used to detect the cars.

_____

(b) Sound effects are used as part of this ride.

Is sound an analogue or digital quantity?

_____

_____

(c) There is an emergency stop button in each car. This sends information back to the main computer which will then stop all other cars which are following on behind.

Why is real time processing necessary in this situation?

_____

_____

(d) Riders cannot control the route they take. These automated vehicles do not run on rails.

Describe another method for guiding an automated vehicle.

_____

_____

_____

_____

(e) Before automated vehicles were used people were employed to drive cars around Dinosaurland.

Give **one** advantage to the owners of the theme park of the cars being automated.

_____

_____

9. (continued)

(f) During the ride people can look at a black and white map of Dinosaurland, which is displayed on a monitor within the car.

(i) Explain how the computer stores a black and white image in memory.

_____

_____

(ii) Using your answer to the question above, how would you expect the following shape to be stored in the computer's memory? Complete Diagram B using binary numbers.

Diagram A: Image displayed on screen

Diagram B: Image stored in computer's memory

(g) Suggest **one** way in which this ride could be simulated in other theme parks.

_____

_____

_____

[END OF QUESTION PAPER]

[BLANK PAGE]

[BLANK PAGE]

FOR OFFICIAL USE

C

KU   PS

Total Marks

0560/403

NATIONAL
QUALIFICATIONS
2006

THURSDAY, 11 MAY
10.35 AM – 12.20 PM

COMPUTING STUDIES
STANDARD GRADE
Credit Level

Fill in these boxes and read what is printed below.

Full name of centre

Town

Forename(s)

Surname

Date of birth

Day Month Year   Scottish candidate number   Number of seat

Read each question carefully.

Attempt **all** questions.

Write your answers in the space provided on the question paper.

Write as neatly as possible.

Answer in sentences wherever possible.

Before leaving the examination room you must give this book to the invigilator. If you do not, you may lose all the marks for this paper.

SCOTTISH
QUALIFICATIONS
AUTHORITY

SA 0560/403 6/14070

©

KU	PS

1. Pupils and staff at Kulross Academy are about to move into a purpose-built, brand-new school.

(a) It was designed using the latest **CAD** technology to enable the designers to view the school from inside and out using a *virtual reality simulation*.

(i) What do the letters CAD stand for?

C_____ A _____ D _____

(ii) Write down the names of **two** input devices that would be used specifically in a virtual reality system.

1 _____

2 _____

(iii) Why would a simulation be useful when designing a new building?

_____

_____

_____

_____

(b) Programmers used an *interpreter* during development of the virtual reality simulation program. When development was completed, however, they used a *compiler*.

(i) What are interpreters and compilers used for?

_____

_____

KU margin marks: 1 0, 2 1 0, 1 0

PS margin marks: 1 0

1. **(b)** **(continued)**

(ii) Why might programmers use an interpreter first, and then on completion use a compiler?

_____

_____

_____

_____

**2
1
0**

(c) The completed program was distributed **by post** to parents, pupils and staff, to allow them to preview the school before building work began.

(i) What distribution medium is most likely to have been used?

(Tick (✓) **one** box.)

CD-ROM ☐   *USB flash drive* ☐   *Floppy disk* ☐

**1
0**

(ii) Explain why the other two media are not suitable.

1 _____

_____

2 _____

_____

**2
1
0**

[**Turn over**

2. At the opening ceremony, guests were given a demonstration of the school's technological facilities.

(a) Distributed throughout the school are *terminals* showing the school's intranet. *Hyperlinks* and *hotspots* are activated using the mouse pointer.

   (i) What is a "hyperlink"?

_____

_____

   (ii) How can users tell that the intranet page has hotspots?

_____

_____

(b) All desktop and laptop computers are networked throughout the school. The network is a *client-server* network.

   (i) What is a client in a network?

_____

   (ii) What is the purpose of a server in such a network?

_____

_____

(c) Some computers within the school are linked to the server via *wireless* technology, while others are connected to the server using cables.

   (i) State **one** advantage of using cables.

_____

_____

   (ii) State **one** advantage of using wireless technology.

_____

_____

KU	PS

2.   (c) (continued)

(iii)   Describe **one** disadvantage of the use of wireless technology.

_____

_____

(iv)   All computers in this network have been fitted with a special card that enables communication with the server.

What is this card called?

_____

_____

(d)   The server has a processor, containing a *control unit*, *ALU* and *registers*.

(i)   What is the function of the ALU?

_____

_____

_____

(ii)   What is the function of the registers?

_____

_____

_____

[Turn over

KU	PS

3. Kulross Academy features a unique *mobile robot* that patrols the corridors during lessons, keeping them free of litter.

(a) The designers originally planned to use a *light guidance system* for the robot to 'find' its way along the corridors. However, they decided to use a *magnetic guidance system* with *real-time processing* instead.

(i) What is meant by "real-time processing"?

_____

_____

(ii) Explain why they decided not to use a light guidance system following a painted line on the floor?

_____

_____

_____

(b) The safety of pupils and teachers is extremely important. Each robot is fitted with multiple bump *sensors* which cause the robot to stop if it detects any pressure.

(i) Is this an example of an *intelligent robot*? _____

(ii) Explain your answer.

_____

_____

_____

_____

3.   (continued)

(c) The program controlling the robot was written using a *control language* and is stored in *ROM* within the robot.

(i)   Describe what is meant by a control language.

_____

_____

_____

(ii)   Describe **one** advantage of storing software on ROM.

_____

_____

_____

[Turn over

4. Another new feature of Kulross Academy is the use of identity cards, with all staff being issued with *smart cards*.

(a) Which of the following statements are true: (Tick (✓) **two** boxes only.)

1. Smart cards have their own processor. ☐

2. It is easy to forge smart cards. ☐

3. Smart cards are also known as mark sense cards. ☐

4. The information on a smart card can be updated. ☐

(b) When they are first issued with smart cards, teachers have to enter a 4-digit pin number. *Verification* is carried out at this stage.

(i) What is the purpose of verification?

_____

_____

(ii) How could the 4-digit pin number be verified?

_____

_____

(c) Pupils use magnetic stripe cards for registration and payment of school lunches. When a pupil enters a classroom, the card is passed through a special piece of hardware.

What is this hardware called?

_____

(d) When a pupil 'purchases' food from any of the school's dining facilities, details of the purchase are logged in a database on the school's computer network.

(i) Many dining staff may be accessing this database at one time.

What is the term used to describe such a database?

M _____ U _____ Database

4.   (d) (continued)

    (ii) Data can be accessed in two ways – *randomly* or *sequentially*. Which type of access would be appropriate in this situation? Explain your answer.

        Type _____

        Explanation _____

        _____

        _____

        _____

  (e) The school's computer network holds lots of personal data about both staff and pupils. The *data controller* must make sure that the data is accurate and kept up to date.

    (i) Describe **two** other responsibilities that the data controller has.

        1 _____

        _____

        2 _____

        _____

    (ii) The *data subjects* also have rights. Who are the data subjects in this case?

        _____

        _____

[Turn over

KU	PS
	2
	1
	0
2	
1	
0	
	1
	0

KU	PS

5. A competition was held to design a new crest for the school. The winning entry is shown below:

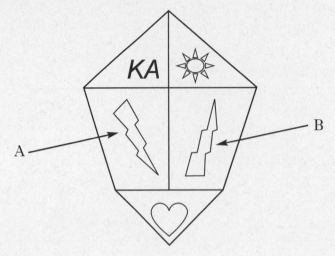

(a) Object A of the image has been copied to create object B.

Describe what else has happened to the copied image.

_____

_____

1
0

(b) The image is scanned and part of the image is *cropped*.

Explain what is meant by cropping a graphic.

_____

_____

1
0

(c) The image is stored as a *black and white bit-mapped graphic*, measuring 450 pixels wide by 600 pixels high.

Calculate the storage requirements in kilobytes.

(Show all working.)

_____

_____

_____

_____

_____

3
2
1
0

5.   (continued)

(d) The graphic is to be distributed electronically to **all** teachers throughout the school. This can be done in two ways:

1. Sent as an *attachment* using electronic mail.

2. Stored in a read/write shared area of the network that teachers and pupils can access.

   (i) What is an attachment?

   _____

   _____

   (ii) Describe **one** advantage of sending the graphic as an attachment.

   _____

   _____

   (iii) Describe **one** disadvantage of distributing the graphic using the shared area.

   _____

   _____

[Turn over

KU	PS

6. A Maths teacher at Kulross Academy uses a spreadsheet to store his pupils' test results. Part of the spreadsheet is shown below:

	A	B	C	D	E	F
1	Name	Test1	Test2	Test3	Average	Letter home?
2	Ben Adams	53	67	63	61	No
3	Paula Bryant	35	33	31	33	Yes
4	Nasim Collins	76	81	93	83	No
5	Darren Daly	23	56	18	32	Yes
6	Lucy Locke	78	72	86	79	No

(a) Cell E2 contains a *function* to calculate the average. It has been *replicated* from E2 into cells E3 to E6.

   (i) What is meant by replication?

   _____

   _____

   (ii) Has *relative* or *absolute* replication been used in this case?

   Explain your answer.

   Type of Replication _____

   Explanation _____

   _____

   _____

(b) The teacher is concerned with the progress of some of his pupils. If a pupil's average result is less than 50, then he intends to send a letter home informing parents of his concern.

   Cell F2 contains a function that automatically identifies the pupils. Part of the function is shown below. Complete the function.

   = _____ (E2 < 50, "Yes", _____)

Margin marks: 1 0 ; 1 0 ; 1 0 ; 2 1 0

6. **(continued)**

(*c*) The Maths teacher finds it time consuming having to create lots of similar letters. His colleague, a Computing teacher, recommends he creates a *standard letter*.

She suggests that the original letter can be scanned into the computer using *OCR*.

  (i) What is meant by "OCR"?

    O_____ C _____ R _____

  (ii) What is a standard letter?

    _____

    _____

  (iii) What is the process called when information from a data file is inserted into a standard letter?

    _____

  (iv) A *template* could also be used to speed up creation of the letters.

    What is a "template"?

    _____

    _____

(*d*) The Computing teacher also recommends that the finished letter is stored as an *RTF* file format.

  (i) What is meant by "RTF"?

    R_____ T _____ F _____

  (ii) Describe **one** advantage of storing a file as an RTF file type.

    _____

    _____

    _____

Margin marks: 10 · 210 · 10 · 210 · 10 · 10

[Turn over

KU	PS

7. The *Network Manager* at Kulross Academy keeps a database of all computer software in the school. Part of the database is shown below.

Kulross Academy - Software Inventory

Name	Date of Purchase	Location	Computer ID	Type
DT Publishing	05-11-05	ICT Rm 1	333	Freeware
DT Publishing	05-11-05	ICT Rm 2	456	Freeware
DT Publishing	10-01-06	ICT Rm 2	342	Freeware
WordPlus	20-05-05	CDT Rm 32	654	Shareware
WordPlus	20-05-05	CDT Rm 32	765	Commercial
WordPlus	20-05-05	CDT Rm 32	875	Shareware
WYNIP	03-04-06	ICT Rm 2	458	Shareware
WYNIP	03-04-06	ICT Rm 1	567	Shareware

(*a*) It has been sorted, in a complex way, on three fields.

Identify the fields in the **order** in which the sort occurs. The first one has been done for you.

FIELD 1. Name

FIELD 2. _____

FIELD 3. _____

2
1
0

(*b*) The network manager wishes to produce a list of all Shareware that was installed before the 1 April 2006. Describe how this could be done.

_____

_____

_____

_____

3
2
1
0

(*c*) Many databases make use of *computed fields*. When would a computed field be used in a database?

_____

_____

1
0

KU	PS

7.   **(continued)**

(d) What is *shareware*?

_____

_____

_____

1
0

(e) What is *freeware*?

_____

_____

_____

1
0

(f) Sometimes pupils try to install games, without permission, on to the school network.

State the name of the piece of legislation which makes this action illegal.

_____

_____

1
0

[Turn over

KU	PS

KU | PS

8. At the end of their first year at Kulross Academy, some pupils decide to create a multimedia presentation highlighting the successes of the new school.

(*a*) The name of the school as well as the new crest will appear in the same position on every slide of the presentation, as shown below.

OUR NEW SCHOOL

Kulross Academy   1.

**Opened: 12th May 2005
by Lady A. Lovelace**

Kulross Academy   2.

Explain how this could be done.

_____

_____

_____

_____

1
0

(*b*) The presentation will also contain sound and other images.

(i) State **one** way of *capturing audio* for the presentation.

_____

_____

1
0

(ii) State **one** way of *capturing images* for the presentation.

_____

_____

1
0

(*c*) What makes this presentation *multimedia*?

_____

_____

_____

1
0

[END OF QUESTION PAPER]

[BLANK PAGE]

FOR OFFICIAL USE

G

KU   PS

Total Marks

0560/402

NATIONAL   WEDNESDAY, 2 MAY   **COMPUTING STUDIES**
QUALIFICATIONS   G/C 9.00 AM – 10.15 AM   **STANDARD GRADE**
2007   F/G 10.20 AM – 11.35 AM   General Level

Fill in these boxes and read what is printed below.

Full name of centre

Town

Forename(s)

Surname

Date of birth

Day   Month   Year   Scottish candidate number   Number of seat

Read each question carefully.

Attempt **all** questions.

Write your answers in the space provided on the question paper.

Write as neatly as possible.

Answer in sentences wherever possible.

Before leaving the examination room you must give this book to the invigilator. If you do not, you may lose all the marks for this paper.

SCOTTISH
QUALIFICATIONS
AUTHORITY

©

DO NOT
WRITE IN
THIS MARGIN

KU	PS

1. The Gibson family are going on holiday to a Scottish island.
    They are travelling by car and ferry.

    (a) The family find out more about the ferry crossing by going *on-line* at
    www.scotferry.co.uk.

    What does the "www" stand for at the beginning of the address?

    W _____ W _____ W _____

    1
    0

    (b) The ferry company sends the Gibsons a letter confirming their booking.
    At the bottom of the letter is a *standard paragraph*.

    What is a standard paragraph?

    _____

    _____

    _____

    2
    1
    0

    (c) The company's stationery looks like this:

    Scotland by Ferry
    Ship Road
    Ullapool

    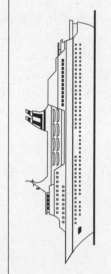

    State the changes that have been made to the graphic at the top to make it
    look like the one at the side.

    _____

    _____

    2
    1
    0

1. (continued)

(d) Throughout the letter, Gibson has been typed as "Gibbson".

What feature of the word processing package could be used to correct this mistake in **one operation**?

_____

(e) The ferry company has enclosed details of its crossings.

Journey	Departure	Arrival
Ullapool – Stornoway	0900	1130
Ullapool – Summer Islands	1030	1110

State **two** advantages in using the *table* facility to create this layout.

1 _____

_____

2 _____

_____

[Turn over

2. The Ferry Company keep a spreadsheet for each crossing.

	A	B	C	D	E	F
1	Ferry Crossings 2007					
2						
3	Journey	Number of passengers	Cost per passenger	Number of cars	Cost per car	Total from passengers and cars
4	Ullapool to Stornaway	300	£13.00	98	£23.00	£6,154.00
5	Ullapool to Summer Islands	150	£7.50	30	£15.00	£1,575.00
6	Oban to Mull	60	£8.00	52	£20.00	£1,520.00
7						
8						
9	Average number of cars per sailing			60		

KU | PS

(a) Cell F4 contains a formula. Part of it is shown below. Complete the formula.

= (_____ * _____) + (_____ * _____)

2
1
0

(b) Cell D9 contains a function. Part of it is shown below. Complete the function.

= _____ (_____ : _____)

2
1
0

(c) State **two** ways in which cell A3 has been formatted.

1 _____

2 _____

2
1
0

(d) What *attribute* has been applied to the numbers in cells C4 to C6?

_____

1
0

KU	PS

3. One of the children in the Gibson family gets seasick on ferry journeys. Mrs Gibson notices that her local chemist has an *expert system*, which covers various illnesses including travel sickness.

(a) What is an expert system?

_____

_____

_____

2
1
0

(b) State **one** area, other than medicine, where an expert system could be used and what it could be used for in that **area**.

Area _____

What it would be used for _____

_____

_____

2
0

(c) On board the ferry there is a *multimedia* presentation about the island.

   (i) State **one** reason for using *audio* in a presentation.

_____

_____

1
0

   (ii) A *hyperlink* is used between slides in the presentation.

    What is a hyperlink?

_____

_____

1
0

   (iii) On one of the islands it is possible to go white water rafting. The presentation includes this as a *video* clip.

    State **one** reason for using a video clip in a presentation rather than a photograph.

_____

_____

1
0

[Turn over

4. (*a*)   The ferry company uses a *database* to keep a file of all its customers. For each of the fields below state a suitable *field type*.

The first one has been done for you.

Field Name	Example	Field Type
Name	Harry Gibson	Text
Address	3 Ballater Drive	_____
Age	36	_____
Outward Journey	13/10/07	_____

(*b*)   Below is part of a record from the customer file.

Name	Harry Gibson
Customer Code	HG3679
Departure	Ullapool
Destination	Stornoway
Outward Journey	13/10/07
Time	1830 hours
Type of Car	Land Ranger

The ferry company wishes to know how many Land Rangers are travelling from Ullapool to Stornoway on 13/10/07.

Choose **five** words from the list below to complete the paragraph.

Search   *Sort*   *Name*   *Stornoway*   *Ullapool*

Destination   *AND*   *13/10/07*   *OR*

Perform a complex _____ on

fields Departure equals _____

AND _____ equals Stornoway

_____ Outward Journey equals _____

AND Type of Car equals Land Ranger.

4. **(continued)**

(c) The company now wish to put this list in alphabetical order

•   firstly by name

•   and then by type of car.

Number the steps below to show the correct order.

☐   and choose to sort on type of car

☐   start a new complex sort

☐   choose to sort on customer name

2
1
0

(d) When a customer's code is typed in, the computer checks that only six characters have been entered.

What *type of check* is this?

_____

1
0

(e) Only certain employees should have access to the database.

Describe **two** suitable methods which they could use to control access.

1 _____

_____

2 _____

_____

2
1
0

(f) A passenger is surprised to receive a brochure from a holiday homes company which is based on the island they are travelling to.

Tick (✓) **one** box which indicates how the holiday homes company got their name and address.

The passenger wrote to the company   ☐

The ferry company have sold their customer list   ☐

1
0

[Turn over

KU | PS

5. The ferry has *sensors* on its doors which prevents the ferry from sailing if the doors are not sealed.

(*a*) (i) State the type of processing that is being used to control the ferry doors.

_____

(ii) State a reason for this.

_____

_____

(*b*) State a type of sensor which could be used in this situation.

_____

(*c*) The ferry sometimes has to transport cargo. Before loading, the cargo is kept in a warehouse. The warehouse uses automated vehicles which are guided by a light system.

Using **some** of the words below complete the paragraph about a light guidance system.

control   feedback   sensor   magnet   instructions

A _____ follows a white line. Should the vehicle move

away from the line _____ causes the computer to send

out _____ which bring it back to the correct position.

(*d*) State **two** advantages of using automated vehicles.

1 _____

_____

2 _____

_____

6. (a) Some people are very frightened of sailing. Describe how *virtual reality* could be used to overcome their fears.

_____

_____

_____

_____

(b) The shop on board the ferry uses a computer program for stock taking. It is written in a *high level language*.

Tick (✓) **two** boxes which are *common features* of high level languages.

Written in binary   ☐

English like   ☐

Portable   ☐

Cannot be edited   ☐

(c) Explain why it is necessary for high level languages to be translated.

_____

_____

_____

(d) How are numbers represented in a computer?

Tick (✓) **one** box.

ASCII   ☐

Pixels   ☐

Binary   ☐

[Turn over

6. (continued)

(e) The shop saves information onto *backing storage*. Put the following types of backing storage into order, according to their *capacity*. One box has been completed for you.

Use **1** for the **smallest** and **4** for the **largest**.

USB Flash Drive   2

DVD Rewriteable   ☐

Hard Drive   ☐

CD Rewritable   ☐

(f) The shop needs to make printouts of its stock taking. The printouts will include figures which must be able to be read clearly.

   (i) Suggest a suitable type of printer.

   _____

   (ii) State **one** reason for your answer.

   _____

   _____

(g) Some passengers like to have a picture of themselves put onto a sheet of paper which shows the ferry and a map of the island.

Number the steps below from 1 to 4 to show the correct order of how this could be achieved. The **first step** should be **numbered 1.**

Import photograph to desk top publishing package   ☐

Print document   ☐

Take photograph of customer with digital camera   ☐

Save document   ☐

KU	PS

6. **(continued)**

(h) Within the shop there is a *monitor* which displays live pictures, with sound, of what is happening on the captain's bridge.

State **two** pieces of hardware, other than a monitor, which could be used to display the live pictures.

1 _____

2 _____

(margin: PS 2 1 0)

(i) The manageress of the shop often uses a *laptop* computer.

State the type of monitor a laptop would have.

_____

(margin: KU 1 0)

(j) The manageress uses her laptop to create adverts for the shop. Complete the following sentences using the words provided.

data   *program*

The manageress uses a desk top publishing package.

This is a _____ file.

With this she creates an advert. This is a _____ file.

(margin: KU 2 1 0)

[Turn over

KU	PS

7. (a) Working out how many cars could travel on the ferry used to be done manually. Now a computer program calculates it.

Who would have examined the old system to see if computerisation was possible? Tick (✓) **one** box.

Programmer ☐

Systems Analyst ☐

Engineer ☐

Network Manager ☐

(b) Use **some** of the following words to complete the sentences below.

programmer   engineers   network manager   systems analyst

When computers were first installed at the ferry company's head office

they were installed by _____ .

A _____ was employed to write a program which

calculates the weight on board the ferry.

There are now so many computers linked together it is necessary to

employ a _____ to allocate usernames.

(c) (i) Some customers pay for their ferry crossing using cheques which have *MICR (Magnetic Ink Character Recognition)* data printed on them.

State **one** advantage of MICR

_____

_____

(ii) Others use *EFT* to pay for their fare.

What do the initials EFT stand for?

E _____ F_____ T _____

Margin marks: 1 0, 2 1 0, 1 0, 1 0

8. (a) The following statements refer to *broadband* or *dial-up* connections.

Choose the appropriate type of connection for each statement.

The first one has been done for you.

	Broadband	**Dial-up**
1 Provides faster speed of access to the Internet.	✓	
2 This type of connection is always on.		
3 This type of connection can be paid for by the minute.		
4 Telephone calls can be made and received at the same time as being connected to the Internet.		

3
2
1
0

(b) What does it mean to be *off-line*?

_____

_____

1
0

(c) The ferry company sends an *e-mail* to a customer which is written in CAPITAL LETTERS.

Why should they **not** have used capital letters?

_____

_____

1
0

(d) On board each ferry there is a *wireless Local Area Network*.

State **two** advantages of using wireless technology.

1 _____

_____

2 _____

_____

2
1
0

[END OF QUESTION PAPER]

[BLANK PAGE]

STANDARD GRADE | CREDIT

2007

[BLANK PAGE]

FOR OFFICIAL USE

KU   PS

Total Marks

C

0560/403

NATIONAL
QUALIFICATIONS
2007

WEDNESDAY, 2 MAY
10.35 AM – 12.20 PM

COMPUTING STUDIES
STANDARD GRADE
Credit Level

Fill in these boxes and read what is printed below.

Full name of centre

Town

Forename(s)

Surname

Date of birth

Day Month Year   Scottish candidate number   Number of seat

Read each question carefully.

Attempt **all** questions.

Write your answers in the space provided on the question paper.

Write as neatly as possible.

Answer in sentences wherever possible.

Before leaving the examination room you must give this book to the invigilator. If you do not, you may lose all the marks for this paper.

SCOTTISH
QUALIFICATIONS
AUTHORITY

KU	PS

1.   Glencoe House is an outdoor centre that provides courses for a wide range of outdoor sports and activities. Details of the courses are found on the centre's website, part of which is shown below.

Rock Climbing

Rock Climbing is one of the most popular activities run by the centre. Click on the links below for more information.

(*a*)   The web page on Rock Climbing includes a series of images as well as an audio voice-over. Some of the images have been *cropped*.

   (i)   What happens to an image when it is cropped?

   _____

   _____

1

0

   (ii)   State **one** method of *capturing images* for a web page.

   _____

   _____

1

0

   (iii)   State **one** method of *capturing audio* for a web page.

   _____

   _____

1

0

KU	PS

1.   (continued)

(b) Access to the Internet is provided by an Internet Service Provider (ISP).

State **two** facilities that the ISP may offer to Glencoe House.

1 _____

_____

2 _____

_____

2
1
0

(c) When potential clients contact Glencoe House, the response sometimes includes an *attachment* saved as a *standard file format*.

(i)   What is an attachment?

_____

_____

1
0

(ii) Name **one** standard file format

_____

1
0

(iii) Describe **one** advantage of using standard file formats.

_____

_____

_____

1
0

[Turn over

KU	PS

2. When clients make a booking, Mirrah, the centre's secretary, enters their details in a database.

(a) Mirrah has poor eyesight. State **two** ways in which her computer's *HCI* could be customised to enable her to carry out this task effectively.

1 _____

_____

2 _____

_____

Part of the database design is shown below.

Field Name	Type	Size	Validation	Sample Record
Client Code	Number	4	>0 and <9999	1342
Surname	Text	20		Astley
Firstname	Text	20		Mike
Address	Text	30		34 Brampton Rd
Town	Text	20		Barnsley
Postcode	Text	8		YK3 7HJ
Sex	Text	6		Male
Date of Birth	Date	6		03/11/78
Course Name	Text	20		Orienteering

(b) A *validation* check is shown. Name the type of validation used.

_____

(c) Describe the difference between *validation* and *verification*.

_____

_____

_____

_____

2. **(continued)**

(d) The centre's database currently holds information concerning 15,000 clients.

Calculate how many **bytes** will be required to store **all** records. (Show your working.)

_____

_____

_____

(e) Mirrah wants to produce a paper copy of all females who have booked the mountain biking course.

(i) Describe how this could be done.

_____

_____

_____

_____

(ii) In this example, is Mirrah a *data subject, data controller* or *data user*?

_____

(iii) Describe **two** rights that a data subject has with the *Data Protection Act*.

1 _____

_____

2 _____

_____

(f) Many databases make use of *computed fields*. What is a computed field?

_____

_____

[Turn over

KU | PS

3. Derek Summers is a programmer.

(*a*) Derek's programs have to be translated into *machine code* before processing can take place. This can be done using either an *interpreter* or *compiler*.

Which type of translator would Derek use in the following situations? Explain why.

(i) While developing the program: _____

Reason _____

_____

_____

_____

2
1
0

(ii) When the program is finished: _____

Reason _____

_____

_____

_____

2
1
0

(*b*) Derek always tries to make sure his software is *portable*. Explain why he does this.

_____

_____

_____

1
0

3.   (continued)

(c) Most of Derek's software is *commercial*. Some of it is *shareware*.

(i) What is shareware?

_____

_____

_____

(ii) Why do you think Derek distributes his work as shareware?

_____

_____

_____

(d) Some of Derek's customers download his software, while others receive their copies by post.

State **one** reason why Derek may prefer his customers to download his software.

_____

_____

_____

(e) All of Derek's software includes *on-line help* and *on-line tutorial* facilities.

Which of these facilities should new customers use when they first receive the software? State **one** reason for your answer.

Facility _____

Reason _____

_____

_____

[Turn over

4. Derek enjoys river kayaking in his spare time. He is keen to extend his skills and has enrolled on a course of sea kayaking at Glencoe House.

(*a*) A week before the course is due to begin, he receives a *standard letter* confirming his place on the course.

(i) What is a standard letter?

_____

_____

_____

_____

(ii) Apart from a word processor, what other application is usually involved in the creation of standard letters?

_____

(iii) State the name of the process that inserts information from this application into the word processed document.

_____

(*b*) On arrival at the centre, Derek is given a *magnetic stripe card* to access his accommodation. To enter his room, he must pass the card through a special piece of hardware.

What is this hardware called?

_____

(*c*) Derek finds an *expert system* providing advice on activities, particularly useful.

Describe **two** advantages of using expert systems.

1 _____

_____

2 _____

_____

KU	PS

4. **(continued)**

(*d*) The centre has a *client-server* network.

(i) State **two** advantages for the centre of using a client-server network.

1 _____

_____

2 _____

_____

(ii) What piece of hardware will have to be installed in each computer to allow access to the client-server network?

_____

(*e*) The centre is considering installing a *wireless* network. State **one** disadvantage of a wireless network in this situation.

_____

_____

_____

(*f*) The manager of the centre used to travel to Glasgow to attend a meeting with other outdoor centre managers. They now use *video conferencing* instead.

(i) State **one** input device required to use video conferencing.

_____

(ii) State **one** advantage to the managers of using video conferencing instead of attending their monthly meeting.

_____

[Turn over

DO NOT
WRITE IN
THIS MARGIN

KU	PS

5. Before heading out on his first sea kayaking activity, Derek uses a *virtual reality simulation* to practise the techniques.

(*a*) Apart from practising new techniques, suggest **two** other reasons why simulators are used by learners.

1 _____

_____

2 _____

_____

(*b*) When he uses the kayak simulator, sensors on the paddle detect the direction of movement and force used. This information is processed and a large *TFT* monitor displays the results of Derek's efforts.

(i) What type of converter will be needed **before processing** of the information can take place? Tick (✓) **one** box only.

D to A converter ☐   A to D converter ☐

2
1
0

1
0

KU	PS

5. (b) (continued)

(ii) The program controlling the kayak is stored on *ROM*. State **two** advantages of storing software on ROM.

1 _____

_____

2 _____

_____

**2
1
0**

(iii) What does TFT stand for?

T _____ F _____ T _____

**1
0**

(iv) State **one** other example of an output device that could be used specifically in a virtual reality system.

_____

**1
0**

[Turn over

KU	PS

6. At the end of the course. Derek prepares to depart.

(a) During the activity, several black and white photographs were taken of Derek and the other clients. He wishes to take copies of them home using his *USB flash drive*.

   (i) He has only 3 Mb of storage space left on his flash drive. Each photograph measures 800×800 pixels. How many photographs can be stored on his flash drive?
(Show all working.)

   (ii) The *operating system* is involved in transferring the images from the computer to the flash drive. State **two** functions of an operating system.

(b) Derek pays for his course by *Electronic Funds Transfer* (*EFT*) using his *smart card*.

   (i) Describe **one** advantage of using a smart card.

   (ii) What are the main stages involved in EFT?

7. The centre uses a spreadsheet to keep track of its clients' accounts. Part of the spreadsheet is shown below.

	A	B	C	D	E
1	**Name**	**Total Cost**	**Discount**	**Amount Paid**	**Money Due**
2	Dino Mancini	520	52	300	168
3	Isla Sutherland	800	80	700	20
4	Sparky Douglas	280	0	200	80
5	Jack Valman	350	0	350	0

(a) Cell C2 contains a *function* that determines any discount due to the client. If a client spends £500 or more on a course, then a discount of 10% is given, otherwise they receive no discount.

Part of the function is shown below. Complete the function.

= _____ (B2>=500, _____, 0)

(b) This function has been replicated from cell C2 into cells C3 to C5. What type of reference has been used?

Type of reference _____

Explain your answer _____

_____

_____

(c) At the end of each month, course directors receive a word processed report containing bar charts showing the number of clients completing their courses and the amount of money due. This information changes from month to month.

What type of linkage has taken place between the word processor and the spreadsheet applications?

Type of linkage _____

Explain your answer _____

_____

_____

[Turn over

7.   (continued)

(d) The client bookings database is a *multi-user* database.   It is password protected in an attempt to prevent unauthorised access and hacking.

(i) What piece of legislation makes this activity an offence?

_____

(ii) What other activity is outlawed in this legislation?

_____

(iii) What type of access would be suitable in this situation – *random* or *sequential*?

Type of access _____

Explain your answer _____

_____

_____

[*END OF QUESTION PAPER*]

STANDARD GRADE | GENERAL

2008

[BLANK PAGE]

FOR OFFICIAL USE

G

	KU	PS
Total Marks		

0560/402

NATIONAL   MONDAY, 12 MAY
QUALIFICATIONS 10.20AM – 11.35AM
2008

COMPUTING STUDIES
STANDARD GRADE
General Level

Fill in these boxes and read what is printed below.

Full name of centre

Town

Forename(s)

Surname

Date of birth

Day	Month	Year		Scottish candidate number		Number of seat

Read each question carefully.

Attempt **all** questions.

Write your answers in the space provided on the question paper.

Write as neatly as possible.

Answer in sentences wherever possible.

Before leaving the examination room you must give this book to the invigilator. If you do not, you may lose all the marks for this paper.

1. Saunders High School are raising money for charity. Ben has entered the money raised from a "car washing" event in the spreadsheet below.

	A	B	C	D	E
1	**Car Washing**				
2					
3		**Feb**	**Mar**	**Apr**	**Best Month**
4	Andrew	£10.70	£3.50	7.1	£10.70
5	Arif	£2.00	£1.10	9	£9.00
6	Hassan	£7.10	£3.20	1.82	£7.10
7	Michael	£6.40	£8.30	2.3	£8.30
8	Christine	£5.80	£6.10	3	£6.10
9					
10				**Average**	**£8.24**

(a) The values in column D have to be formatted to look like those in columns B and C.

Describe how this can be done.

_____

_____

_____

_____

(b) In cells **E4** and **E10** functions have been used.
Complete the following.

(i) E4 =_____ (____ : ____)

(ii) E10 =_____ (____ : ____)

1. (continued)

(c) Cells E4 to E8 each contain a formula. This formula was only entered once in cell E4

    (i) Describe how this formula was *replicated*.

    (ii) Ben wants to stop people from changing his formulae. Explain what feature he must use to stop this happening.

(d) The headteacher would like to see the figures displayed as a bar chart but he is not familiar with the package. State the feature of the package that could help him.

(e) The file is saved to a small portable device.

    (i) What is the name of this device?

    (ii) State whether the file saved is an *application file* or a *data file*.

    (iii) Explain the difference between an application file and a data file.

2. A library uses a database to hold the details of all of its books.

(*a*) A sample record is shown below.

Field Data	Sample Data	Field Type
Book Title	Treasure Island	Text
Cover	Treasure Island A Novel by Robert Louis Stevenson	A
Author	Robert Louis Stevenson	Text
ISBN	0448058251	B
Due to be returned	22/06/08	C
Keywords	Pirate, treasure, adventure, gold	Text

Identify the **field types** which are listed as A, B and C.

A = _____

B = _____

C = _____

(*b*) A *check digit* is used to ensure data is entered correctly.

(i) State the field in the record above that makes use of a check digit.

_____

(ii) Describe how a check digit is created.

_____

_____

_____

_____

KU | PS

2.   (continued)

(c)   Complete the following search screen to obtain a list of all adventure books written by Scott Miller due to be returned by 30/06/08.

LIBRARY DATABASE SEARCH SCREEN

Book Title	
Author	
ISBN	
Due to be returned	Before 30/06/08
Keywords	

SEARCH

2
1
0

(d)   The librarian's computer is connected to a network which includes all of the libraries in the country.

What type of network is this?

_____

1
0

(e)   State the term used to describe an attempt to gain illegal access to the library's network.

_____

1
0

[Turn over

3. The home page for a local builders' Web site is shown below.

**Aviemore	Torrance	Dennison**	
	This is the most popular design in our range of bungalows. Three bedroom, two bathroom, living room, dining room, kitchen, garage, GCH, DG.
	This is one of the smaller terraced houses. Three bedroom, two bathroom, living room, dining room, kitchen, garage, GCH, DG.
	This is a popular design in our detached house range. Three bedroom, two bathroom, living room, dining room, kitchen, garage, GCH, DG.

(a) When a user clicks on the word "Dennison", they are taken to a new Web page. State the name of this feature.

_____

(b) The image of the first house has been inserted incorrectly.

State **two** changes required to correct this problem.

_____

_____

_____

(c) The text for the web page was created in a *general purpose package*.

State the most suitable type of package for creating the text.

_____

KU	PS

3. **(continued)**

(d) One of the paragraphs has been saved and inserted into the text for each house.

    (i) Name this type of paragraph.

_____

    (ii) State **two** advantages of using a pre-prepared piece of text.

      1 _____

      _____

      2 _____

      _____

(e) A *high level language* was used to create the Web site.

    (i) Name a language that could be used to create Web pages.

_____

    (ii) State **two** common features of high level languages.

      1 _____

      2 _____

    (iii) What characters are used in *machine code*?

_____

(f) The Web site includes many types of *multimedia*. State **one** type and explain how it could be used to improve the Web site.

Type: _____

Explanation:_____

_____

_____

_____

[Turn over

KU | PS

4. Morag uses *on-line banking* to check the balance of her account at ScotWide Bank.

(*a*) Morag has a dial-up connection to the Internet.

(i) State **two** disadvantages of using a dial-up connection.

1 _____

2 _____

(ii) Name another type of connection.

_____

(*b*) Morag cannot remember the Web address of the ScotWide Bank Web site. Using some of the words below, complete the sentences to describe how she can find her bank's Web site.

ScotWide   *engine*   *account*   *browser*

She would load up her _____ to view Web pages.

She would then use a search _____ and enter

_____ Bank.

(*c*) Morag must enter two pieces of information to access her personal account. One of them is her username. State the other piece of information needed.

_____

(*d*) What type of computer is used by the bank to store all of their customer details?

_____

DO NOT
WRITE IN
THIS MARGIN

KU	PS

4. (continued)

(e) When Morag enters her details into her computer they are *encrypted* before being sent to the bank

    (i) State what is meant by the term encrypted.

_____

_____

_____

1
0

    (ii) Explain why her details have to be encrypted.

_____

_____

1
0

(f) Morag's computer system has a LCD monitor. What do the initials LCD stand for?

L_____C_____ Display

2
1
0

[Turn over

KU | PS

5.   CheapWays supermarket has installed a new checkout system.

(a)   When an item is scanned, the price appears on the checkout display. What type of processing is this?

_____

10

(b)   State **one** running cost of the new checkout system.

_____

10

(c)   When a customer pays using a bank card, the money is taken from their account and transferred into the supermarket's bank account.

(i)   State the term used to describe this transfer of money.

_____

10

(ii)   State **one** advantage to the **supermarket** of this type of payment rather than paying with cash.

_____

_____

10

(iii)   State **one** advantage to the **customer** of this type of payment rather than paying by cash.

_____

_____

10

6. A factory currently employs people to make chairs. They are about to introduce an automated system.

(a) State **two** changes that may happen to the jobs of the workers.

1 _____

2 _____

(b) A person is employed to plan the new system.

(i) State the job title of this person.

_____

(ii) Name **two** other computing jobs, excluding the one used above, that might be needed in the factory.

1 _____

2 _____

(c) Use some of the words below to complete the paragraph about the new system.

tool   mobile   feedback

stationary   sensor   robot

When a chair moves along the conveyor belt it is detected by a

_____ which sends _____ to the main

computer. The conveyor belt stops and a robot uses a paint spraying

_____ to paint the chair. This type of robot is called a

_____ robot.

(d) State **two** ways that the robot could have been taught to paint the chairs.

1 _____

_____

2 _____

_____

[Turn over

KU	PS

7. Rebekkah is writing her life story using a word processing package. An extract is shown below.

> Before my trip up the Amazon, I had to make sure that I had the following:
>
> **Checklist**
>
> | **Food** | **Medical** | **Gear** |
> |----------|-------------|----------|
> | Beans | Bandages | Rope |
> | Pasta | Plasters | Knife |
> | Rice | Aspirin | Compass |

(a) Rebekkah uses a spell checker to find mistakes in her document.

  (i) Describe the steps that a spell checker takes when checking a word that is spelt incorrectly.

_____

_____

_____

_____

_____

3
2
1
0

  (ii) The word Amazon is spelt correctly, but was identified as incorrect by the spell checker.

State how you could prevent "Amazon" from being highlighted by the spell checker.

_____

_____

1
0

7. (continued)

(b) Rebekkah notices that throughout her book she has called her friend "McGregor" instead of "MacGregor".

Describe how this could be corrected in a single operation.

_____

_____

_____

(c) Rebekkah wants to record images and sounds on her expedition.

State **two** input devices that she would need.

1 _____

2 _____

[*END OF QUESTION PAPER*]

[BLANK PAGE]

[BLANK PAGE]

C

FOR OFFICIAL USE

KU   PS

Total Marks

0560/403

NATIONAL
QUALIFICATIONS
2008

MONDAY, 12 MAY
1.00 PM – 2.45 PM

COMPUTING STUDIES
STANDARD GRADE
Credit Level

Fill in these boxes and read what is printed below.

Full name of centre

Town

Forename(s)

Surname

Date of birth

Day Month Year   Scottish candidate number   Number of seat

Read each question carefully.

Attempt **all** questions.

Write your answers in the space provided on the question paper.

Write as neatly as possible.

Answer in sentences wherever possible.

Before leaving the examination room you must give this book to the invigilator. If you do not, you may lose all the marks for this paper.

©

KU	PS

1. Bethany owns the Blue Gables Hotel. She is trying to encourage more guests to stay at the hotel.

She sends out *standard letters* offering special deals to people who have stayed in the hotel before. The letters all contain the same information apart from the personal details such as name and address which will be inserted.

(a) Name the process that is described above.

_____

1
0

(b) Before printing the letters, Bethany uses both the *spell checker* and the *grammar checker*.

State an example of a mistake that would be picked up by each of these proofing tools.

Spell Checker _____

2
1
0

Grammar Checker _____

(c) Bethany designs a poster to advertise her hotel.

(i) State a suitable application package for her to use and explain your choice.

Suitable Package _____

Explanation _____

_____

2
0

1. (c) (continued)

(ii) She includes the logo from the Tourist Information Web site on her poster.

Explain why Bethany might be breaking the law by using this graphic.

_____

_____

_____

(iii) State how Bethany could include this logo from the Tourist Information Web site without breaking any laws.

_____

_____

(d) The logo she finally includes is represented in black and white. It contains 267200 pixels in total.

Calculate the storage requirement of this graphic in **kilobytes**. Show all your working.

_____

_____

_____

(e) Bethany also includes one of her own photographs.

She wants to remove part of the picture as shown below.

State the most suitable tool for Bethany to use

_____

Part to be removed

1
0

1
0

2
1
0

1
0

KU	PS

2. "Buzz" is a company which designs and manufactures digital alarm clocks.

Management is currently considering automating the entire process so they employ a *systems analyst*.

(a) Describe **two** tasks the systems analyst will perform.

1 _____

_____

_____

2 _____

_____

_____

**2
1
0**

(b) State **two** economic implications to the company if they go ahead with the systems analyst's recommendations.

1 _____

_____

_____

2 _____

_____

_____

**2
1
0**

(c) When factories are designed for robots they look very different from those designed for humans.

State **two** ways in which they differ.

1 _____

_____

_____

2 _____

_____

**2
1
0**

2. **(continued)**

(d) The digital alarm clocks let you wake up to music playing from an audio CD. The clocks contain a *Digital* → *Analogue converter.*

Explain why the clocks must contain a Digital → Analogue converter.

_____

_____

_____

(e) A digital alarm clock is an example of an *embedded system.*

(i) What is an embedded system?

_____

_____

(ii) State the storage medium used by an embedded system.

_____

[**Turn over**

3. Mohammad is a pupil at Alba Academy. He has broken his ankle and will have to work from home for the next month

His Computing teacher has asked him to research *mobile Internet technologies* and produce a report.

(a) State **two** mobile Internet technologies.

1 _____

2 _____

(b) He uses a *search engine* to help with his research.

What is a search engine?

_____

_____

_____

_____

(c) Mohammad becomes particularly interested in mobile Internet technologies that are manufactured in Japan.

(i) State a *complex* search that he could use in this situation.

_____

_____

_____

(ii) State **one** advantage of using a complex search rather than a simple search.

_____

_____

_____

3. **(continued)**

(*d*) He decides to word process his report and then *e-mail* it to his teacher as an *attachment*.

Mohammad realises that he should save his report using a *standard file format*.

(i) State **two** suitable text formats that he could use.

1 _____

2 _____

(ii) Explain why he should use a standard file format.

_____

_____

(*e*) As well as saving a copy of his report on the *hard disk*, he also saves it on his *USB flash drive*.

State **two** reasons why USB flash drives have become so popular.

1 _____

_____

2 _____

_____

(*f*) Mohammad could also have stored a copy of his report on a CD-RW.

What do the letters CD-RW stand for?

_____

_____

[**Turn over**

4. Rachel works in the administration department of her local college. She types up the students' projects and prints them out.

The college has recently bought a new printer for Rachel.

(*a*) State the piece of software necessary for the printer to work correctly.

_____

(*b*) The *operating system* on her computer has *background job capability*.

Explain why this could be an advantage to Rachel.

_____

_____

_____

_____

(*c*) One function of an operating system is *memory management*.

(i) State how each storage location in memory is identified.

_____

_____

(ii) Name the term used to describe the number of bits stored in each memory location.

_____

KU	PS

4. **(continued)**

(*d*) Another function carried out by an operating system is *file management*.

(i) State the type of filing system used to manage files shown in the diagram below.

_____

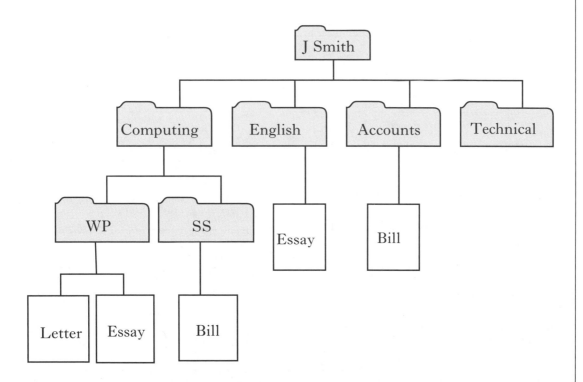

(ii) State **two** reasons for using this type of filing system.

1 _____

_____

2 _____

_____

[Turn over

KU	PS

5.   At the headquarters of a well known bank, a *mainframe computer* system is used to process data.

(a)   (i)   State **two** reasons why it is necessary to use a mainframe computer system in this situation.

1 _____

_____

2 _____

_____

(ii)   Clearly explain the difference between *data* and *information*.

_____

_____

_____

(b)   Most banks have started issuing their customers with *smart cards*.

State **two** reasons for doing this.

1 _____

_____

_____

_____

2 _____

_____

_____

_____

KU | PS

5. **(continued)**

(c) *Validation* and *verification* are two error checking processes.

Complete the table below.

Process	Meaning	Example
validation		Range Check
verification	Making sure that the data is entered correctly	

(d) (i) State **one** reason why banks are keen to promote *on-line banking*.

_____

_____

(ii) Do you think customers are happy with on-line banking?

☐ Yes ☐ No Tick (✔) **one** box.

Explain your answer making **two** clear points

_____

_____

_____

_____

(e) Computers make it easier to collect *management information*.

State **one** example of management information which would be useful to a bank manager.

_____

_____

_____

[Turn over

6. All the best young athletes in the country have been encouraged to attend a special training camp. They will each have three attempts to impress the coaches at their chosen event.

A target is set for each event. To represent their country, the athletes must achieve the target.

Below is part of a spreadsheet set up for the 100 metres sprint.

	A	B	C	D	E	F
1	**100 metres sprint**					
2						
3	**Under 16 Boys**			**Target Time (secs)**		12.8
4						
5	**Name**	**Race 1**	**Race 2**	**Race 3**	**Best Time**	**Represent Country?**
6	R Gracie	12.8	12.9	13.2	12.8	Yes
7	L MacAra	13.1	12.9	12.9	12.9	No
8	H Hunt	12.9	12.9	12.8	12.8	Yes
9	M Dykes	12.9	12.6	12.6	12.6	Yes
10	L Fraser	13.0	13.0	13.0	13.0	No

(a) State the formula that will be used to calculate R Gracie's best time in cell E6.

_____

(b) The formula in cell E6 is copied into cells E7 to E10.

   (i) State the type of *referencing* used. Explain your answer.

   Type _____

   Explanation _____

   _____

   _____

   _____

   (ii) State another word for "copied" when referring to spreadsheets.

   _____

6.   (continued)

(c)   State the type of formula contained in cell F6.

_____

(d)   At the training camp, they are shown a multimedia presentation about the importance of keeping fit.

The presentation includes both *audio* and *video* elements.

State **two** ways that audio can be added to the presentation.

1   _____

_____

2   _____

_____

(e)   The slides in this presentation are linked as shown below.

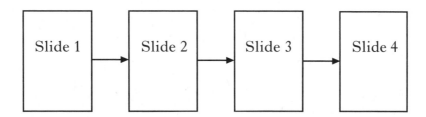

(i)   State the type of linkage used above.

_____

(ii)   Describe a way in which Slide 1 could directly link to Slide 3.

_____

_____

[Turn over

KU PS

6. **(continued)**

(f) At the end of the training camp all athletes are given a copy of the presentation on DVD.

Give **two** reasons why this would be a suitable storage medium.

1 _____

_____

2 _____

_____

(g) The athletes are told about an application package which would make decisions and offer advice about nutrition.

Name this type of package.

_____

2
1
0

1
0

7. A new medical centre has been opened in Bankness.

Computers are used to store the patients' data.

The computers are linked together to form a *Local Area Network* (LAN).

(*a*) The data held about patients is highly confidential.

   (i) Which Act states that data must be kept secure?

   _____

   (ii) State **one** other requirement of this Act when storing personal data.

   _____

   _____

(*b*) One way of keeping data secure is the use of *physical* methods.

   State **two** different physical methods.

   1 _____

   _____

   2 _____

   _____

(*c*) The network in the medical centre is one where many users can share the main computer's resources at the same time.

   (i) State the term used to describe this type of network.

   _____

   (ii) What piece of hardware is required on each of the stations to connect to the network?

   _____

[*END OF QUESTION PAPER*]

[BLANK PAGE]

STANDARD GRADE | GENERAL

2009

[BLANK PAGE]

FOR OFFICIAL USE

G

KU	PS	TOTAL

0560/402

NATIONAL
QUALIFICATIONS
2009

WEDNESDAY, 13 MAY
10.20AM – 11.35AM

COMPUTING STUDIES
STANDARD GRADE
General Level

Fill in these boxes and read what is printed below.

Full name of centre

Town

Forename(s)

Surname

Date of birth

Day	Month	Year

Scottish candidate number

Number of seat

Read each question carefully.

Attempt **all** questions.

Write your answers in the space provided on the question paper.

Write as neatly as possible.

Use **blue** or **black ink**.

Answer in sentences wherever possible.

Before leaving the examination room you must give this book to the invigilator. If you do not, you may lose all the marks for this paper.

KU | PS

1. DC Electronics is developing robots for use in the new UK space program.

The secretary is about to send out a letter to all of the workers.

(a) On looking over the letter the secretary notices that "spice" has been used instead of "space" throughout.

   (i) State the feature of a word processing package, which can be used to make this change in one operation.

   _____   **1**

   (ii) Describe how you would use this feature to correct the spelling of "spice".

   _____

   _____

   _____   **2**

(b) Before printing, the secretary did a *spelling check* of the letter. It highlighted "RobotRanger" each time as wrongly spelled.

   (i) Explain how a spelling check feature works.

   _____

   _____

   _____   **2**

   (ii) State how you would stop this happening again.

   _____

   _____   **1**

(c) After correcting the spelling, there are still some mistakes.

State the feature that would pick up the error shown below.

"The first trial of the RobotRanger <u>are</u> the 12th of June".

   _____   **1**

1. **(continued)**

(*d*) When writing the letter, the secretary makes use of *standard paragraphs*.

State **what** a standard paragraph is.

_____

_____

_____

(*e*) The company decides to alter the letter and produce a newsletter using a *desk top publishing* package instead.

Describe how they can do this **without** re-typing the text of the letter.

_____

_____

(*f*) A picture of the robot designers, shown below, is to be put into the newsletter. The photograph is too large to fit.

State what must be done to make it fit.

_____

(*g*) The secretary has used *tables* **before** but has forgotten how to use them.

She could use *on-line help* or an *on-line tutorial* for assistance.

(i) State which one would be more suitable.

_____

(ii) Explain your choice for the above answer.

_____

_____

[Turn over

DO NOT
WRITE IN
THIS MARGIN

KU	PS

2. Anwar Animations is a firm that writes games programs using a range of different computers such as *palmtops* and *laptops*.

(a) State **one** disadvantage of using palmtop computers for writing programs.

_____

_____   1

(b) Palmtop computers use a special type of screen for input.

Name this type of screen.

_____   1

(c) When programs are edited, the code is stored in *main memory*.

State the type of main memory used.

_____   1

(d) One of the files created when writing the program needs to be used on another computer. The file size is 850 megabytes.

What type of backing storage is required to allow them to move it to another computer?

_____   1

(e) The program is written in a *high level language* but the computer only understands *machine code*.

What needs to happen to the program to allow it to be used on a computer?

_____

_____   1

KU | PS

2. **(continued)**

(f)   Anwar Animations keeps details of its workers on computer.

State **two** rights the workers have to this information.

1 _____

_____

2 _____

_____

(g)   The company uses a *wireless network*.

State **two** reasons for using wireless networks

1 _____

_____

2 _____

_____

2

2

[Turn over

KU | PS

KU | PS

3. Northern Oil stores the parts and suppliers it needs to build oil lines. Part of the information is shown below.

Company Name	Jones Electrics
Address 1	12 High Street
Address 2	Cardonald
Town	Glasgow
Invoice Number	5149542
Order Value	£34,234
Date of Order	25th April 2009

(*a*) Complete the following sentences using the words below.

    file   *record*   *field*

The example shown above is a _____ .

"Invoice Number" is a _____ .

When you save the _____ you are saving all of the information about the parts and suppliers.

3

(*b*) The manager wants a paper copy of **all** orders from Glasgow.

Explain how they could do this.

_____

_____

_____

_____

3

KU | PS

3. (continued)

(c) Northern Oil wants to put its list of parts and suppliers in order of invoice number, largest number first.

Explain how this is done.

3

(d) The company wants to store the details of when the order was delivered.

Explain what alterations are needed to allow this.

1

(e) State **two** *running costs* the company may have when using computers and working with the database.

1 _____

2 _____

2

(f) Much of the day-to-day office work can be done from home using fast Internet links and e-mail.

State two **disadvantages** of working from home rather than working in the office.

1 _____

2 _____

2

[Turn over

KU	PS

4. Look Web is a company that produces websites. They also produce video clips and photos to suit the web pages.

   (a) On a web page you can click on *hyperlinks*.

      (i) State the purpose of hyperlinks.

      _____

      _____

      _____

      1 (KU)

      (ii) State **one** way of identifying hyperlinks on a web page.

      _____

      _____

      1 (PS)

   (b) Look Web and its customers keep in contact by using *electronic mail*.

      (i) State **one** advantage, other than cost, of communicating using electronic mail instead of normal post.

      _____

      _____

      1 (KU)

      (ii) Look Web sent an e-mail with 12 separate attachments. The e-mail was 18 megabytes in size and used capitals throughout.

      This e-mail has broken **two** rules of *netiquette*.

      What are they?

      1 _____

      _____

      2 _____

      _____

      2 (PS)

DO NOT
WRITE IN
THIS MARGIN

KU | PS

4. (continued)

(c) Look Web uses a *search engine* to help in finding information when designing their web pages.

One of their searches was for Glasgow Cross in 1920.

Put a tick (✓) in the box that will give the **best** results.

Glasgow Cross in 1920   ☐

Glasgow Cross and 1920   ☐

"Glasgow Cross" + 1920   ☐

1

(d) The designer used *HTML* to make the website.

What does HTML stand for?

H _____ Text M _____ Language

2

(e) When designing the web pages, Look Web can also add video clips to the pages.

State **one** advantage of adding video clips to a web page.

_____

_____

1

[Turn over

5. Able Art Printing company use spreadsheets as part of its business. A sample is shown below.

	A	B	C	D
1	Able Art Pri			
2				
3	Part No.	Number Ordered	Item Cost	Order Cost
4	AB123	60	£1.00	£60.00
5	CD621	32	£10.50	£336.00
6	HX810	2	£20.05	£40.10
7	GD657	38	3.20	£121.60
8			Total	£557.70
9				
10			Average	£139.43
11				

(a) The name of the company, Able Art Printing, does not fit in the column.

State what must be done to the column to make the name fit.

_____   1

(b) What *cell formatting* has been used in cell B3 so that both words appear?

_____

_____   1

(c) A *formula* is used in cell D8.

Complete the formula

= _____ (_____ : _____)   2

(d) A formula is also used in cell D10.

Complete the formula

= _____ (_____ : _____)   2

(e) The formula for cells D4 to D7 was entered in D4. It was then *replicated* down the column.

State what is **meant** by replicated.

_____

_____   1

KU	PS

5.   (continued)

(f)   State how the *format* of cell C7 should be changed so that it looks the same as cell C6.

_____

_____

(g)   The security of the data is very important.

State **two** methods that could be used to protect data.

1   _____

_____

2   _____

_____

(h)   The company is also worried that its data may be lost.

State what can be done to make sure this data is not lost.

_____

_____

[Turn over

KU	PS

6. SpaceRanger robots are designed to work on Mars.

(a) *Virtual Reality* was used during the design process. Explain what virtual reality is.

_____

_____

_____

2

(b) State **two** reasons why the space program is using robots instead of humans.

1 _____

_____

2 _____

_____

2

(c) An engineering firm building the SpaceRanger uses *mobile robots* to transport parts around the factory.

(i) State **two** safety features that may be required in the factory.

1 _____

_____

2 _____

_____

2

(ii) Mobile robots use *real-time processing* when they detect an object in their path.

Explain why real-time processing is used.

_____

_____

_____

1

KU	PS

6. **(continued)**

(*d*) The finished robots come with a range of sensors.

State **two** types of sensor.

1 _____

2 _____

[Turn over

DO NOT
WRITE IN
THIS MARGIN

KU	PS

7. Jennifer is an artist. She has decided to sell her work in her own shop.

(*a*) People buying goods in her shop can use their credit cards.

Payment is made using *EFTPOS*.

What do the letters POS stand for?

P _____ of S _____

2

(*b*) (i) The items sold in the shop have *bar codes* on them.

State **one** advantage of using bar codes.

_____

_____

1

(ii) Bar codes have *check digits*.

State the purpose of a check digit.

_____

_____

1

(*c*) The shop uses *interactive processing* when items are sold.

What is meant by interactive processing?

_____

_____

1

(*d*) The shop uses a database package to store the details of the goods sold in the shop.

At the end of the day, a new file of all the items sold is created.

Use these words to fill in the blanks.

    database package   *database file*

The _____ _____ is the program file.

The _____ _____ is the complete set of data.

2

[*END OF QUESTION PAPER*]

STANDARD GRADE | CREDIT

2009

[BLANK PAGE]

FOR OFFICIAL USE

KU   PS   TOTAL

C

0560/403

NATIONAL
QUALIFICATIONS
2009

WEDNESDAY, 13 MAY
1.00 PM – 2.45 PM

COMPUTING STUDIES
STANDARD GRADE
Credit Level

Fill in these boxes and read what is printed below.

Full name of centre

Town

Forename(s)

Surname

Date of birth

Day   Month   Year   Scottish candidate number

Number of seat

Read each question carefully.

Attempt **all** questions.

Write your answers in the space provided on the question paper.

Write as neatly as possible.

Use **blue** or **black ink**.

Answer in sentences wherever possible.

Before leaving the examination room you must give this book to the invigilator. If you do not, you may lose all the marks for this paper.

1. PetrolPatrol is a fuel company.

In order to communicate with branches in different countries they use a *Wide Area Network*.

(*a*) (i) Name **one** type of *transmission media* which could be used in a Wide Area Network.

_____

(ii) State the main disadvantage of sending information over a Wide Area Network.

_____

_____

(*b*) A monthly management meeting is held using *video conferencing* facilities.

(i) State **two** advantages **for the company** holding their meetings this way.

1 _____

2 _____

(ii) Each video conferencing room contains a *webcam*. State the purpose of the webcam in this situation.

_____

_____

(*c*) The minutes of the meeting will be sent via e-mail to all the managers. They are highly confidential.

State what should be done to the file before it is sent electronically.

_____

_____

DO NOT
WRITE IN
THIS MARGIN

KU	PS

1. (continued)

(d) One manager asked that details of the meeting were saved using a *standard file format*.

(i) Explain why he made this request.

_____

_____

1

(ii) One standard file format used for word processed documents is *RTF*.

What does RTF stand for?

R _____ **T** _____ **F**ormat

1

(iii) Name another standard file format used for word processed documents.

_____

1

[Turn over

DO NOT
WRITE IN
THIS MARGIN

KU	PS

2. (a) Garage Galore have invested a lot of money in an *expert system* to help with diagnosing faults when servicing cars.

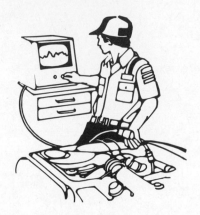

(i) Explain in detail what an expert system is.

_____

_____

_____

_____   2

(ii) State **two** advantages of using an expert system rather than relying on a human expert.

1 _____

_____

2 _____

_____   2

(b) Christabel works in the admin department of Garage Galore. She makes use of information stored about customers to send out individual reminders when their cars are due a service.

(i) State the process that Christabel will use to allow her to produce personal reminders without doing each one individually.

_____   1

(ii) Describe the steps involved in carrying out this process.

_____

_____

_____   3

2.   **(continued)**

(*c*) Christabel gave a list of customer details to a car dealer. He wanted to send out promotional leaflets advertising special offers.

State whether Christabel was right to hand over the customers' details and give **one** reason to justify your answer.

_____

_____

_____

2

(*d*) Draw lines to show the correct relationships in the diagram below.

| Garage Galore | | Data User |

| Christabel | | Data subject |

| Customer | → | Data controller |

2

[Turn over

	KU	PS

3. Classy Computers have asked their sales team to sell as many printers as possible this week. To encourage the sales team, they have offered a bonus in their wages if they sell 90 or more.

The spreadsheet shown below contains the result of the promotion.

	A	B	C	D	E	F
1		**Models of Printer**				
2						
3		**Z331**	**Z361**	**Z391**	**Total**	**Bonus**
4						
5	**Y Pavlova**	34	21	17	72	No
6	**K Rice**	25	45	20	90	Yes
7	**J Hirtzel**	30	39	22	91	Yes
8	**H Scott**	26	36	20	82	No
9	**A Stewart**	35	42	25	102	Yes
10						
11						
12	**No. of printers sold to qualify for bonus**				90	

(a) Complete the formula that would be used in cell F5.

= **IF** (_____E12 , _____ , _____)

3

(b) The formula in cell F5 was replicated down into cells F6 to F9. Both *absolute* and *relative referencing* were used.

Explain carefully why this was necessary

_____

_____

_____

_____

_____

2

(c) The sales team were often asked by customers to recommend a printer that they should buy.

Apart from cost, state **two** factors that the customers should consider when buying a new printer.

1 _____

2 _____

2

KU	PS

4. Charlie would like to help his daughter with her Computing homework. He decides to attend college in the evenings to learn about writing programs.

At the first class the tutor explains that there are a wide variety of *high level languages*.

(a) High level languages need to be translated before they can be executed. State what they are translated into.

_____

1

(b) State **two** other features of a high level language.

1 _____

2 _____

2

(c) *Interpreters* and *compilers* are two examples of translator programs.

Read the following statements and write either **interpreter** or **compiler** in the box at the right hand side to match the description.

A translator that points out your mistakes as you enter your program.

A translator that lets you run your program as fast as possible.

A translator that lets you edit your mistakes easily.

A translator that doesn't need to remain in memory when you run your program.

4

(d) Translator programs are an example of *systems software*.

State **one** other example of systems software.

_____

1

[Turn over

KU | PS

5. The Senior pupils at TreeView Academy are planning to stage six coffee mornings throughout the year. They decide to create a poster giving the details.

(a) One pupil suggests they use a *freeware* program to design the coffee cup.

State what is meant by the term freeware.

_____

_____

_____

2

(b) Another pupil suggests they start by creating a *template*.

(i) State what is meant by a template.

_____

_____

2

(ii) State **one** advantage of using a template.

_____

_____

1

(c) They decide to use a photograph of the school from an old magazine.

State how they can include the photograph in the poster.

_____

1

(d) Once the photograph has been inserted they realise it is necessary to *crop* and *scale* it.

(i) State what it means to crop the photograph.

_____

_____

1

(ii) State what it means to scale the photograph.

_____

_____

1

KU | PS

5.   (continued)

(e)   One of the photographs used was 37 *kilobytes*.

How many *bits* are in 37 kilobytes?

Show all your working.

_____

_____

_____

_____

2

[Turn over

DO NOT WRITE IN THIS MARGIN

KU | PS

6. Nu4Old is a large insurance company that deals with both house and car insurance. It is necessary for them to store details about their clients.

Some of the details for each client are shown below.

Customer Number	Name	Street
2356497289	Alison MacRae	26 Upper Green Street
Town	Postcode	Telephone
Hillytown	HT4 6HM	01536328776
Insurance Type		
House		

(a) Explain why each customer is allocated a customer number.

_____

_____

(b) All telephone numbers have 11 digits. State the type of check carried out to ensure this number is entered correctly.

_____

(c) Nu4Old have over ten million customers. There is a huge amount of information to be processed and stored very quickly.

State the type of computer most likely to be used.

_____

(d) Nu4Old require a random/direct access backing storage medium to store the details about all the customers.

   (i) Name a suitable backing storage medium.

_____

_____

   (ii) Explain why random/direct access would be required.

_____

_____

6.   (continued)

(e) This database of customer details can be accessed by many people at the same time.

State what type of database this is.

_____

1

(f) Kyrre is an employee of Nu4Old. He changed the details of his friend's car to get him a cheaper deal for his car insurance.

(i) Name the Act Kyrre has breached.

_____

1

(ii) State **one** other breach of the Act.

_____

1

[Turn over

7. Fabien has been storing information about his travels using a database package.

The format of a record in his database is shown on the right.

Field Name	Sample Data
Country	Belgium
Capital	Brussels
Area (km²)	30528
Population (millions)	10·5
Last Visited	12/05/07
Population Density	334

(a) Name **two** different data types stored in this record.

1 _____

2 _____

(b) Fabien decides to add another field to his database. The new field will contain a picture of each country's flag.

State the data type of this new field.

_____

(c) Fabien wants to find out how many countries he has visited in the year 2000 which have a population of more than 5 million. He realises that he will need to carry out a *complex search* to produce this list.

(i) Explain what is meant by a complex search.

_____

_____

(ii) Describe the steps he should take to produce this list.

_____

_____

_____

_____

(d) Fabien has used a *computed field* to calculate the population density.

Explain what is meant by a computed field.

_____

_____

8. Factories often use *mobile robots* to carry heavy components from one place to another.

(a) (i) Describe **two** different methods of guiding these mobile robots along their routes.

Method 1 _____

_____

_____

_____

Method 2 _____

_____

_____

_____

(ii) Give **one** advantage for each of the methods you have described.

Advantage of Method 1 _____

_____

_____

Advantage of Method 2 _____

_____

_____

_____

[Turn over

8.   (continued)

(b) The factory manager realises that new automated equipment is expensive.

(i) State **two** arguments that the factory manager could use to persuade the company to invest in new automated systems.

1 _____

_____

2 _____

_____

(ii) He decides to buy *intelligent robots*.

Name **two** hardware features of an intelligent robot.

1 _____

_____

2 _____

_____

2

2

[*END OF QUESTION PAPER*]

STANDARD GRADE | GENERAL

2010

[BLANK PAGE]

FOR OFFICIAL USE

G

KU	PS	TOTAL

0560/402

NATIONAL
QUALIFICATIONS
2010

MONDAY, 10 MAY
10.20AM – 11.35AM

COMPUTING STUDIES
STANDARD GRADE
General Level

Fill in these boxes and read what is printed below.

Full name of centre

Town

Forename(s)

Surname

Date of birth

Day   Month   Year   Scottish candidate number

Number of seat

Read each question carefully.

Attempt **all** questions.

Write your answers in the space provided on the question paper.

Write as neatly as possible.

Use **blue** or **black ink**.

Answer in sentences wherever possible.

Before leaving the examination room you must give this book to the Invigilator. If you do not, you may lose all the marks for this paper.

1. Matthew has just started college.

(a) He wants to buy a computer that he could use when he is in the lecture hall taking notes.

   (i) State the **type** of computer he should buy.

   _____

   1

   (ii) State **one** reason for your choice of computer.

   _____

   _____

   1

(b) No matter where he is in the college grounds, Matthew can connect to the *Internet* using his new computer.

   State how his laptop is able to do this.

   _____

   _____

   1

(c) While using the word processor to write an essay he mistakenly used the same word twice.

   "... ... the the ... ..."

   Name the feature of the word processing program that would highlight this error.

   _____

   1

1. (continued)

(d)   The essay is 12 pages long. Throughout the essay he misspelled MacDonald as McDonald.

  (i)   Name the feature of the word processing package that could be used to correct this in a single operation.

_____

  (ii)   Describe how he would use this feature to correct the names.

_____

_____

_____

(e)   Matthew only wants to print the last three pages of his essay.

State how he could do this.

_____

_____

_____

(f)   One of the other programs Matthew makes use of is a spreadsheet. The word processor and spreadsheet have a *common HCI*.

State **one** reason why a "common HCI" is useful.

_____

_____

_____

[Turn over

2. Colour Metals produce special metal work for house builders.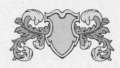

They pay their workers a basic weekly wage plus an overtime amount if they work any extra hours for the week. Part of their spreadsheet used to work out the weekly wage is shown below.

	A	B	C	D	E
1	Name	Basic Wage	Overtime worked	Hourly Rate for overtime	This Weeks Pay
2					
3	Black, D	200	5	£17·00	£285·00
4	Hussein, D	176	12	£14·00	£344·00
5	Smith, F	150	10	£12·00	£270·00
6	Wong, L	220	15	£19·50	£512·50
7					
8				Total	£1,411·50

(a) A formula is used in cell E3 to work out the wage.

Complete the formula.

= _____ + (_____ * _____)

2

(b) Cell E8 also contains a formula.

Complete the formula.

= _____ (_____ : _____)

2

(c) Describe how you would change the cells in column B to make them look like column D.

_____

_____

2

KU	PS

2. **(continued)**

(d) A new employee has joined the company and their information has to be added to the spreadsheet shown on *Page four*.

Explain how you would add "Harrison, J" to the sheet in the correct location.

_____

_____

_____

2

(e) A new assistant in the office has been asked to keep the spreadsheet up to date. They use an *online tutorial*.

State why they would use an online tutorial.

_____

_____

1

(f) State how the assistant could display the information in the table in a more easily understood format.

_____

1

(g) The company used a graphics program to design their logo.

Version 1   Version 2

State **two** features of the graphics program used to change Version 1 into Version 2.

1 _____

2 _____

2

[Turn over

3. A company sells its own furniture designed with the help of computers and built by robots.

(a) One of the reasons that the company uses robots is because they are more *efficient* than human workers.

State **two** reasons why robots are more efficient than human workers.

1. _____

_____

2. _____

_____

2

(b) A robot is used to carry furniture around the warehouse.

(i) State the **type** of robot used.

_____

1

(ii) This type of robot often uses a *magnetic guidance system* to move around the warehouse.

Describe how this magnetic guidance system works.

_____

_____

_____

2

(c) When planning a new piece of furniture, the company runs a *simulation* before programming the robots.

State **one** reason why a simulation would be used.

_____

_____

1

3. **(continued)**

(d) The robots can pick up a chair without damaging it.

Explain how this can be achieved.

_____

_____

_____

_____

(e) When designing the furniture, the company makes use of an **input device** which allows them to create detailed drawings.

Name this input device.

_____

[Turn over

2

1

4. Carol works for a travel agent and they use a database to store the holiday details.

Examples of the details held on the database are shown below.

Field name	Example data
Country	Spain, France, USA
Type of holiday	All inclusive, bed and breakfast, room only, camping
Location	Orlando, Las Americas, Paris, Amsterdam
Number in party	12, 3, 1
Date	12/7/2010
Duration	7 days, 10 days

(*a*)   A family of 3 people would like to go on a 5 day holiday to Spain. They want to stay in a hotel in Barcelona from 21/9/2010.

Complete the following screen to find a list of suitable holidays.

Country	
Type of holiday	Hotel
Location	
Number in party	3
Date	21/9/2010
Duration	

3

KU	PS

4. **(continued)**

(b)   Complete the sentences using some of the words below.

   text   *search*   *date*   *sort*   *numeric*

   (i)   When Carol looks for a country that a family wants to visit, she will

   _____ the database.

   (ii)   A_____ field type is used to store the "Number in party".

   (iii)   Carol would _____ the database to put the locations into alphabetical order.

(c)   Carol sends out the final details of the holidays to the family two weeks before their holiday is due to start. She makes use of *standard paragraphs* when creating the letters.

   (i)   State what a standard paragraph is.

   _____

   _____

   (ii)   State **one** advantage to Carol of using standard paragraphs.

   _____

   _____

   _____

(d)   The travel agent has a website that customers can use to help find a holiday that suits them. It uses an *expert system* to provide suggestions.

   State what is meant by an expert system.

   _____

   _____

[Turn over

5. A shop sells electrical equipment. Sales are stored on a computer.

Each item has a unique numeric code.

(a) State **two** possible checks that could be carried out on the code to make sure it is valid.

1. _____

_____

2. _____

_____   2

(b) The shop makes use of both *data* and *information*.

Describe what is meant by:

Data: _____

_____

Information: _____

_____   2

(c) Complete the sentences using some of the words below.

programmer   engineer   systems analyst   network manager

(i) The _____ can recommend new software or hardware.   1

(ii) The _____ maintains the computer system.   1

(iii) The _____ maintains user access on the computer network.   1

(d) When a purchase is made in the shop, customers pay using a card. This is processed by EFT.

Fill in the missing words

Electronic F_____ T_____   2

KU	PS

5. (continued)

(e) Customers are worried that their personal details could be altered or lost.

(i) State the name given to the process of gaining unauthorised access to information.

_____

1

(ii) State **two** methods that could be used to protect data stored on computers.

1. _____

_____

2. _____

_____

2

[Turn over

KU | PS

6. A new fire safety system, including software and hardware, is being installed.

(*a*) Programs for the system are written in a *high level language*.

They need to be *translated* before use.

   (i) State **two** features of a high level language

      1. _____

      _____

      2. _____

   (ii) The programs are translated into *machine code*.

      State what is meant by machine code.

      _____

      _____

2

1

(*b*) The new fire safety system will make use of either a *real-time* or an *interactive system*.

   (i) State which one would be used.

      _____

   (ii) Give **one** reason for your choice in part (i).

      _____

      _____

1

1

(*c*) The program for the new fire safety system could be stored on a DVD-RW.

Fill in the missing words.

D_____ V_____ Disk Re-Writeable.

2

6. **(continued)**

(*d*)   Memory can be measured in *megabytes*.

   (i)   State the number of *kilobytes* that make up a megabyte.

_____   1

   (ii)   State the number of *bits* that make up a *byte*.

_____   1

(*e*)   What does the word *bit* stand for?

_____   2

[Turn over

7. A club is going to buy some new computer equipment.

(a) They want to buy a printer. They have to take certain features into account.

Tick (✓) **one** feature that is **not** relevant to printers.

Resolution	
Pixel size	
Speed	

1

(b) They are also going to buy a laptop computer. It makes use of a *GUI* and has an *LCD* screen.

Fill in the missing words.

(i) G_____ U _____ Interface   2

(ii) Liquid C _____ Display   1

(c) They are looking at buying a palmtop computer.

State **two** possible input devices that could be used with a palmtop.

1. _____

2. _____   2

(d) One use of the laptop is making *multimedia* presentations.

(i) State the meaning of the term multimedia.

_____

_____   1

(ii) State a method of getting their photographs into the laptop.

_____   1

[END OF QUESTION PAPER]

[BLANK PAGE]

FOR OFFICIAL USE

C

KU	PS	TOTAL

0560/403

NATIONAL
QUALIFICATIONS
2010

MONDAY, 10 MAY
1.00 PM – 2.45 PM

COMPUTING
STUDIES
STANDARD GRADE
Credit Level

Fill in these boxes and read what is printed below.

Full name of centre

Town

Forename(s)

Surname

Date of birth

Day	Month	Year

Scottish candidate number

Number of seat

Read each question carefully.

Attempt **all** questions.

Write your answers in the space provided on the question paper.

Write as neatly as possible.

Use **blue** or **black ink**.

Answer in sentences wherever possible.

Before leaving the examination room you must give this book to the Invigilator. If you do not, you may lose all the marks for this paper.

1. The *spreadsheet* below shows an order placed with the Delicious Delights Cake Company.

	A	B	C	D
1	**Delicious Delights Cake Company**			
2				
3	**Invoice Number**	**8767**		
4				
5	**Item**	**Number**	**Price per cake**	**Cost**
6				
7	Fairy Cakes	36	£0·35	£12·60
8	Tiffin	72	£0·45	£32·40
9	Pineapple Cakes	50	£0·60	£30·00
10	Date Slices	40	£0·75	£30·00
11	Flapjacks	80	£0·50	£40·00
12	Custard Creams	40	£0·60	£24·00
13				
14			Total Cost	£169·00
15			Discount	£16·90
16			Final Cost	£152·10

(a) The *cell protection* feature of the spreadsheet package is used frequently.

   (i) State what is meant by "cell protection".

   _____

   _____

   (ii) Name **one** cell in the above spreadsheet it would be sensible to protect.

   _____

(b) The *formula* to calculate the cost of Fairy Cakes is in cell D7.

   State the **range** of cells this formula has been replicated into.

   _____

1. (continued)

(c) State the type of referencing used when the formula in D7 was replicated. State **one** reason for your answer.

Type of referencing _____

Reason _____

_____

_____

(d) The discount is calculated as follows.

If the Total Cost of the order is greater than £100 then a discount of 10% is given. If not, they do not get a discount.

State the formula that was entered in cell D15.

= IF (_____ , _____ , _____)

(e) State the formula that was entered in cell D16 to calculate the Final Cost.

_____

[Turn over

2. Hannah has just finished taking part in a work experience programme at school. She has to write a two page report describing what she has enjoyed most.

(a) Hannah notices that her report is spread over three pages.

State **two** ways that Hannah can ensure her report is only two pages long.

1 _____

_____

_____

2 _____

_____

_____

(b) When editing her report Hannah makes regular use of the *toolbar* and *keyboard shortcuts*.

(i) State what is meant by the term "toolbar".

_____

_____

_____

(ii) State **one** advantage to Hannah of using keyboard shortcuts.

_____

_____

_____

(c) Before saving her report Hannah adds her name and date as a *footer*.

Explain what is meant by the term "footer".

_____

_____

_____

2

1

1

2

2. (continued)

(d) She decides to *e-mail* a copy of the report to the company she was working with.

State what you call a file that is sent along with an e-mail.

_____

_____

1

(e) When the company opens Hannah's file they find they cannot read it.

State **one** reason why they cannot read the file.

_____

_____

_____

1

[Turn over

3. Bartek is the manager of a company which has recently introduced a network of desktop computers into its offices.

(a) One of the benefits of using the network has been the improved *flow of information* around the office.

Explain **two** ways in which the network has helped improve the flow of information.

1 _____

_____

_____

2 _____

_____

_____

2

(b) Bartek had to choose between running an *integrated package* and *a software suite* on the new desktop computers.

State **one** similarity and **one** difference between an integrated package and a software suite.

Similarity _____

_____

_____

Difference _____

_____

_____

2

3. **(continued)**

(c) Bartek has a secretary with poor eyesight. Describe **two** ways the *HCI* can be customised to make it easier for the secretary to use a computer.

1 _____

_____

_____

2 _____

_____

_____

(d) Other health issues exist when people use computers frequently.

(i) Apart from eye strain, state **one** other health issue that Bartek might be concerned about.

_____

_____

(ii) State what Bartek could provide to prevent the health issue you have chosen in part (i).

_____

_____

[Turn over

KU	PS

4. Monique has bought a new *laptop* to take with her to university in Dundee.

(*a*) (i) Name **one** input device, other than a *keyboard*, that is built into the laptop.

_____

1

(ii) The laptop has a *TFT* screen. State what the initials TFT stand for.

_____

1

(iii) The laptop can read CD-ROMs. These have a storage capacity of 750 *megabytes*.

Calculate how many *bits* there are in 750 megabytes. **(Show all working.)**

_____

_____

_____

_____

_____

3

(*b*) Monique checked that her laptop also contained a *sound card*.

State what feature of the sound card would let her listen to music using audio CDs.

_____

_____

1

4. (continued)

(c) Monique plans to use her laptop for doing research on the *Internet*.

(i) State the **type** of site on the Internet designed to help you find information.

_____

1

(ii) She uses it to look for any drama clubs in Dundee.

State the type of *search* she will use.

_____

1

(iii) Write down exactly what you think Monique will enter to find a list of drama clubs in Dundee.

_____

_____

_____

2

(d) Monique gets a list of names and addresses of seven drama clubs in Dundee. She sends a letter to each asking for part time work.

She plans to write one basic letter with placeholders for personal details.

(i) State the name for this type of letter.

_____

1

(ii) State the name for the operation which will insert the personal details into the placeholders in her letter.

_____

1

[Turn over

KU | PS

5. An automated system has been installed in a bottle manufacturing plant. Each *robot* on the production line is linked to a computer.

(a) (i) Name the type of language used when writing programs for automated systems.

_____

1

(ii) Explain why this type of language is used.

_____

_____

_____

1

(b) The software for the robots on the production line can be held either on a disk or in ROM.

State **one** advantage of disk based software.

_____

_____

1

(c) Some of the robots on the production lines can be considered as **intelligent**.

Describe **two** features a robot must have to be considered intelligent.

1 _____

_____

2 _____

_____

2

(d) The bottle manufacturing plant uses *mobile robots* to transfer heavy materials around the factory.

Humans work in the same area as the robots. State **two** possible *safety precautions* which should be in place.

1 _____

_____

2 _____

_____

2

6. (a) The *processor* is made up of three components.

Fill in the blanks in the table below.

Component	Description
Control Unit	
	Carries out calculations and makes simple comparisons
Registers	

(b) Describe how the processor distinguishes between memory locations.

_____

_____

_____

(c) State how text is **represented** in computer systems.

_____

All computers require an *operating system*.

(d) State **two** functions of an operating system.

1 _____

_____

2 _____

_____

[Turn over

7. Seonag has created a website to advertise her holiday cottage on a Scottish island.

(a) (i) Seonag used web page creation software to produce her website.

State the language that Seonag used to create her website.

_____

1

(ii) State the type of software needed to view her website.

_____

1

(b) Most web page creation packages make use of *wizards* and *templates*.

(i) Explain why using a wizard is helpful to a beginner.

_____

_____

_____

2

(ii) State what is meant by the term "template".

_____

_____

_____

2

Her website allows users to connect with other websites.

(c) State what Seonag has done to allow this to happen.

_____

_____

1

7. (continued)

(d) Seonag also added a *table* showing pictures and details of local tourist attractions.

(i) State **one** advantage of using a table for this purpose.

_____

_____

_____

The table included *hotspots*.

(ii) State how anyone browsing the website will know where the hotspots are on the page.

_____

_____

_____

[Turn over

KU | PS

8. BookBliss is a mail order company dealing in second hand books.

Interactive processing is used when a customer orders a book.

(a) (i) State what is meant by the term "interactive processing".

_____

_____

1

(ii) State **one** advantage to the customer and **one** advantage to BookBliss of interactive processing.

Customer _____

_____

BookBliss _____

_____

2

(b) State what *backing storage medium* should be used to store the company's stock list. Justify your choice.

Backing Storage Medium _____

Justification _____

_____

_____

2

(c) When not dealing with its main job of serving customers, the computer system processes the staff payroll.

State the name given to this type of task.

_____

1

8. (continued)

(d) Each employee in BookBliss has an employee number. Part of this number is a *check digit*.

Explain how a check digit is used to detect errors.

_____

_____

_____

2

(e) Bookbliss has its own small computer department. They employ *programmers*, an *engineer* and a *network manager*.

Choose **two** of the jobs mentioned above and give a description of what would be involved.

   (i) Name of Job _____

      Job Description_____

      _____

1

   (ii) Name of Job _____

      Job Description_____

      _____

1

(f) BookBliss has been approached by another bookseller asking to buy its customer list. BookBliss refuses to do this claiming it is illegal.

State which law would be broken.

_____

1

[END OF QUESTION PAPER]

[BLANK PAGE]

[BLANK PAGE]

[BLANK PAGE]

[BLANK PAGE]

[BLANK PAGE]

[BLANK PAGE]

[BLANK PAGE]